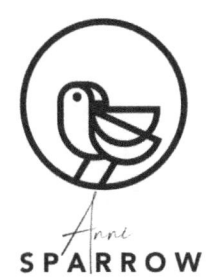

Anne
SPARROW

Dot to Dot
experience

JOURNEY THROUGH
ASIA AND PACIFIC

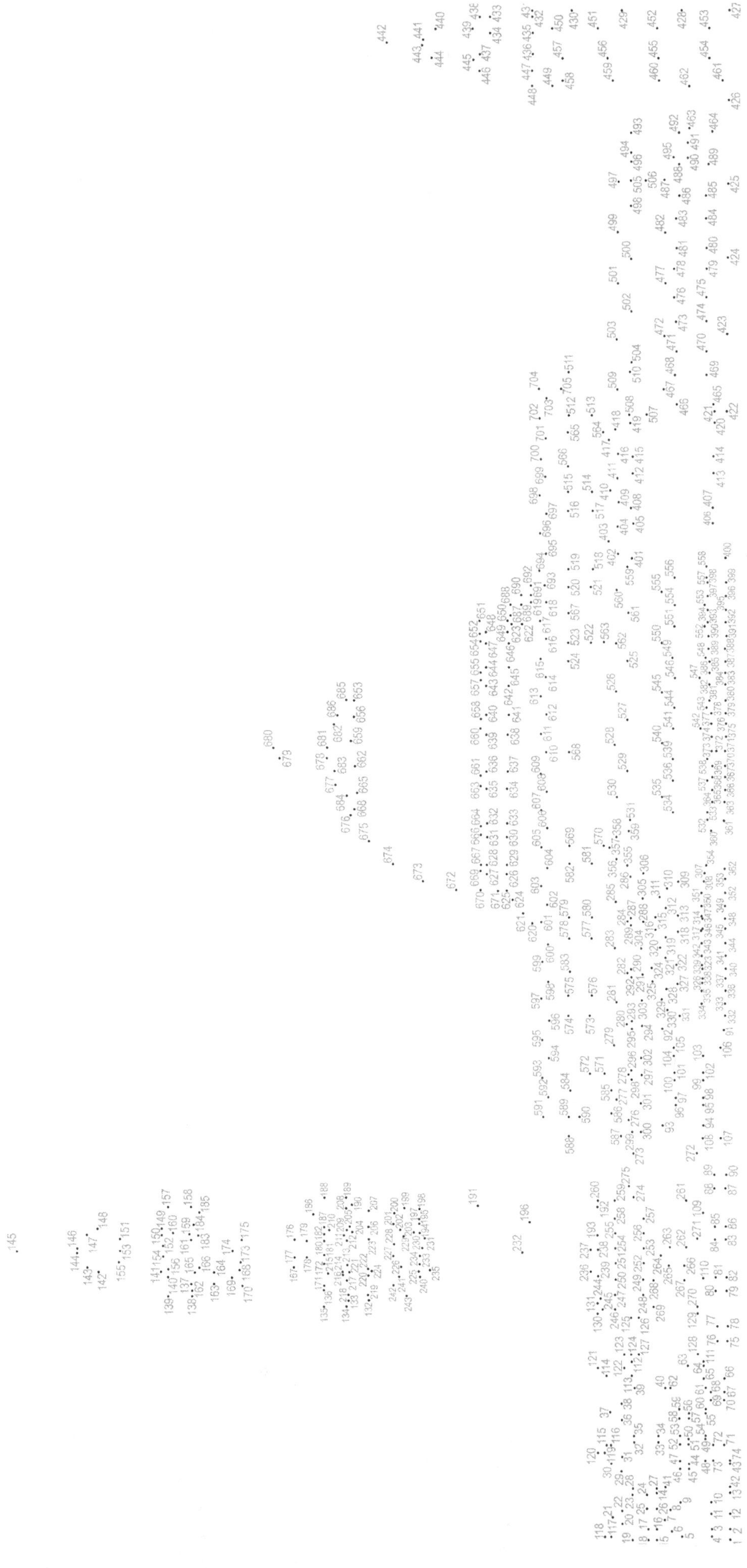

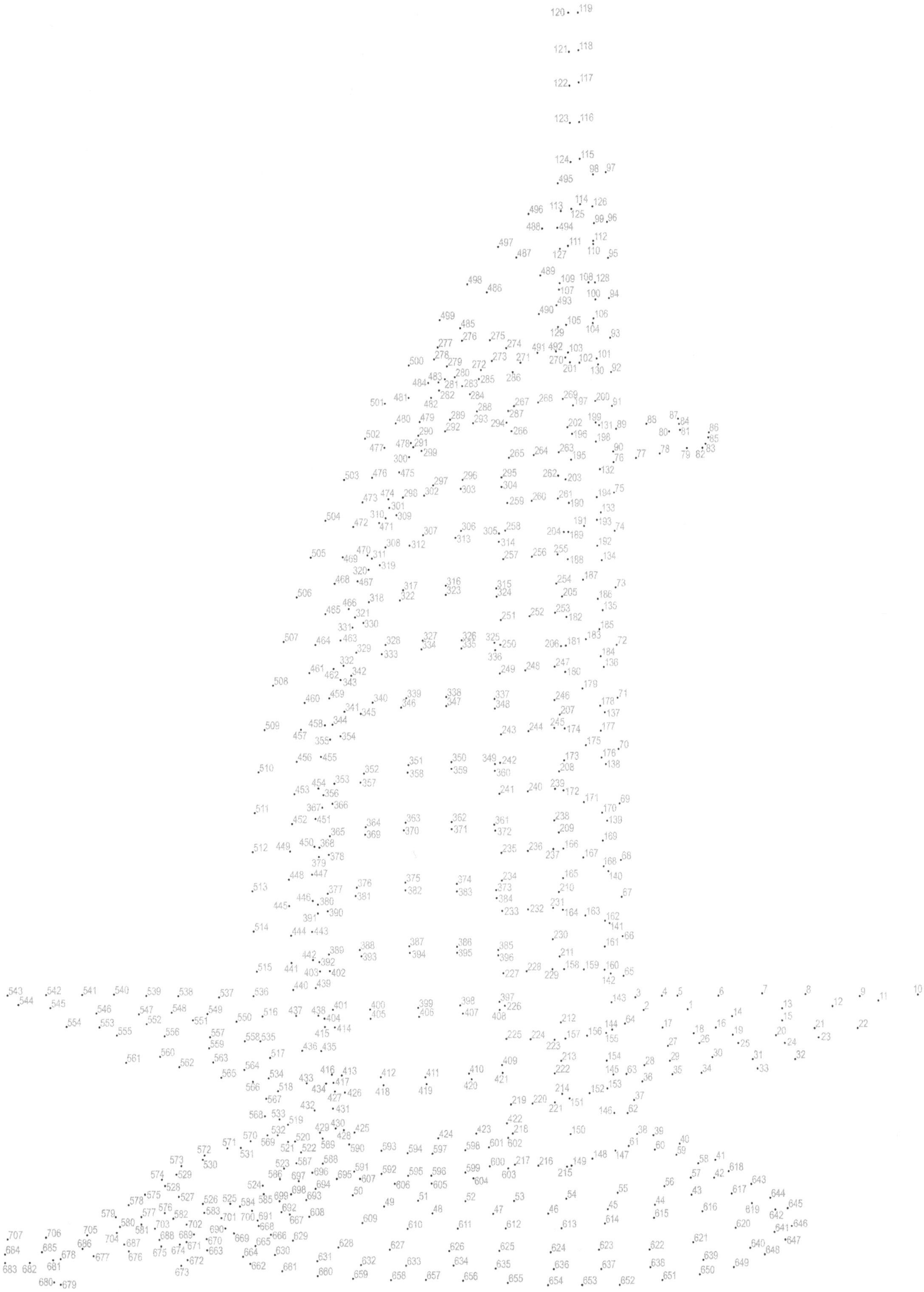

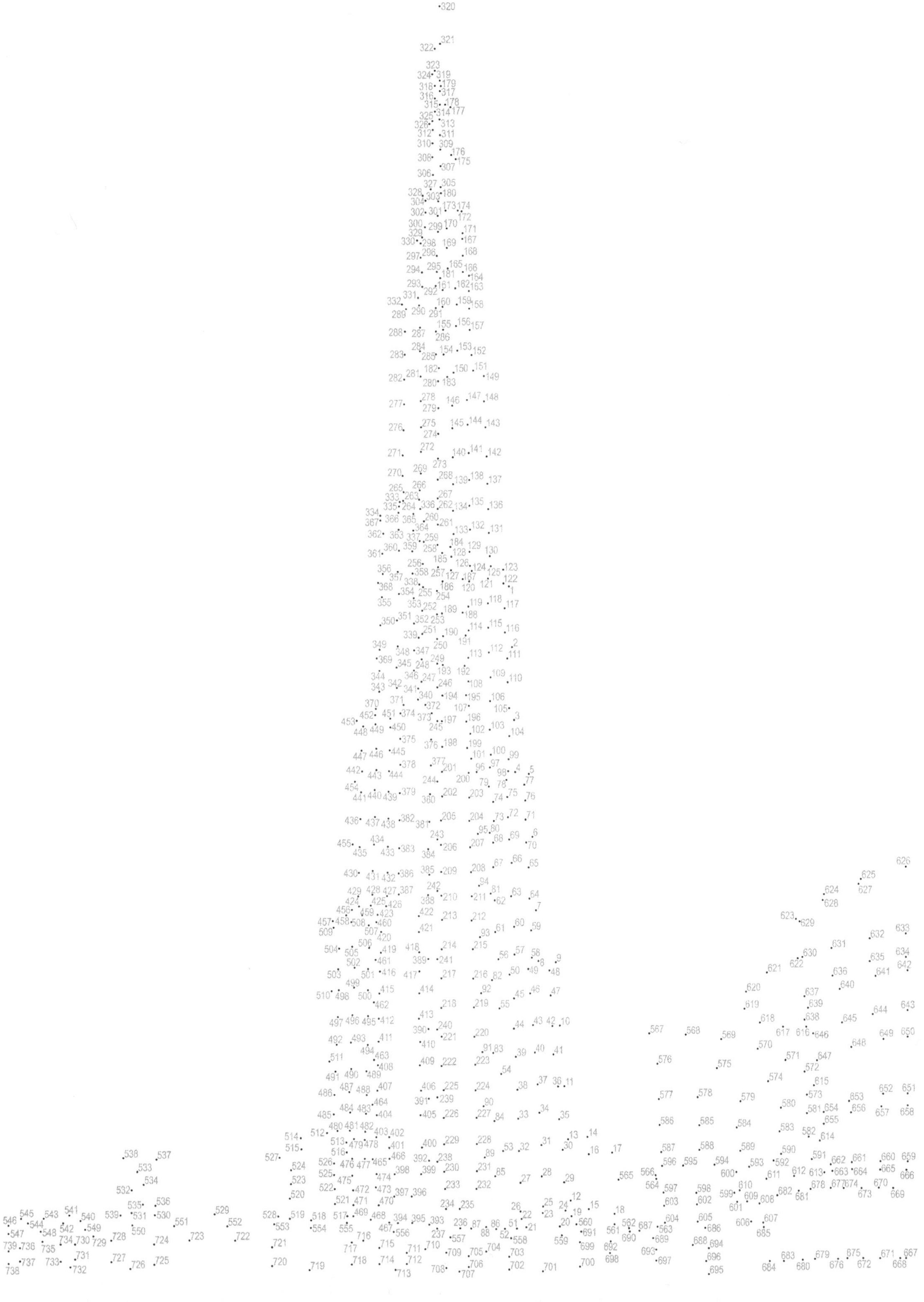

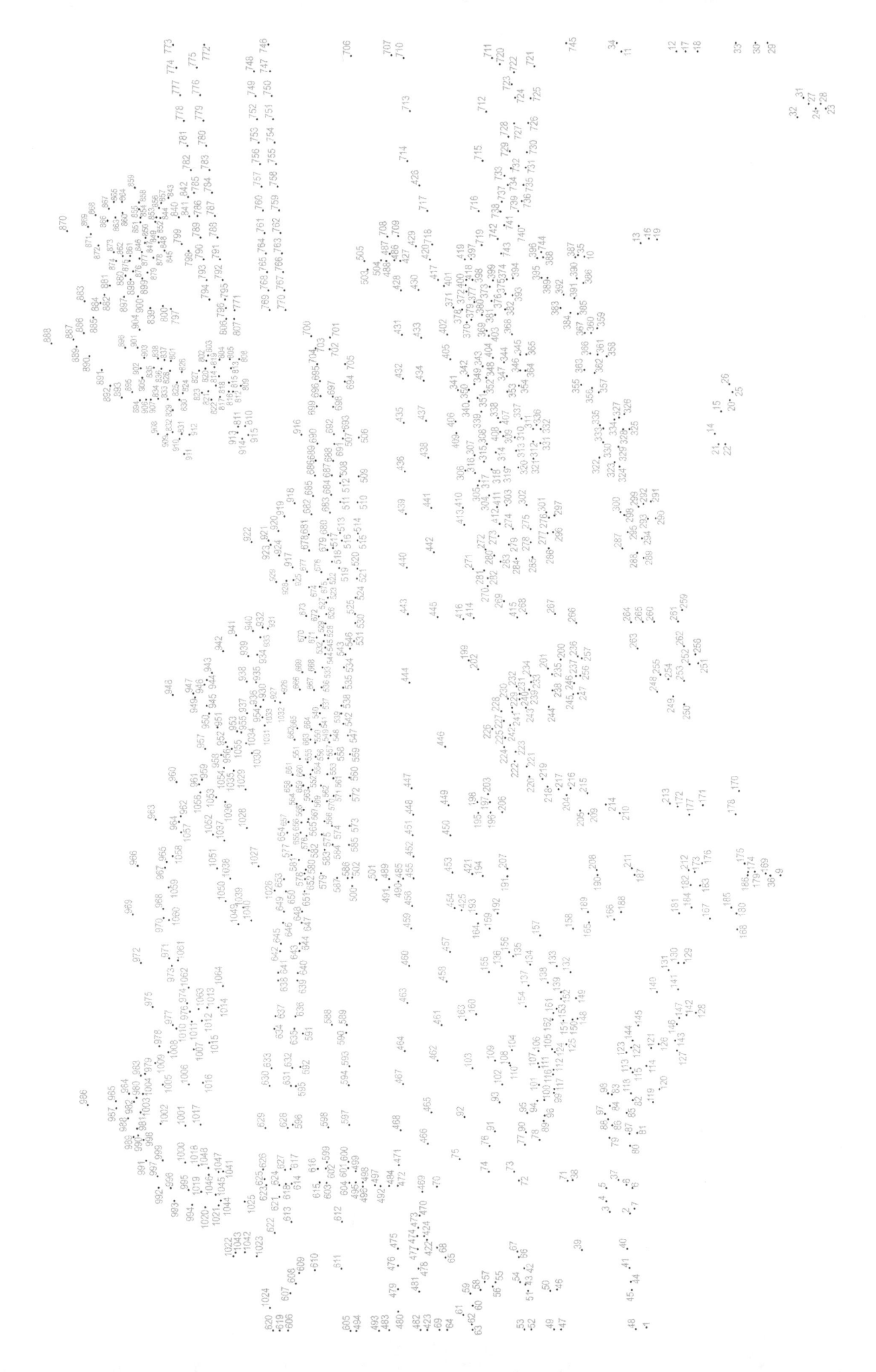

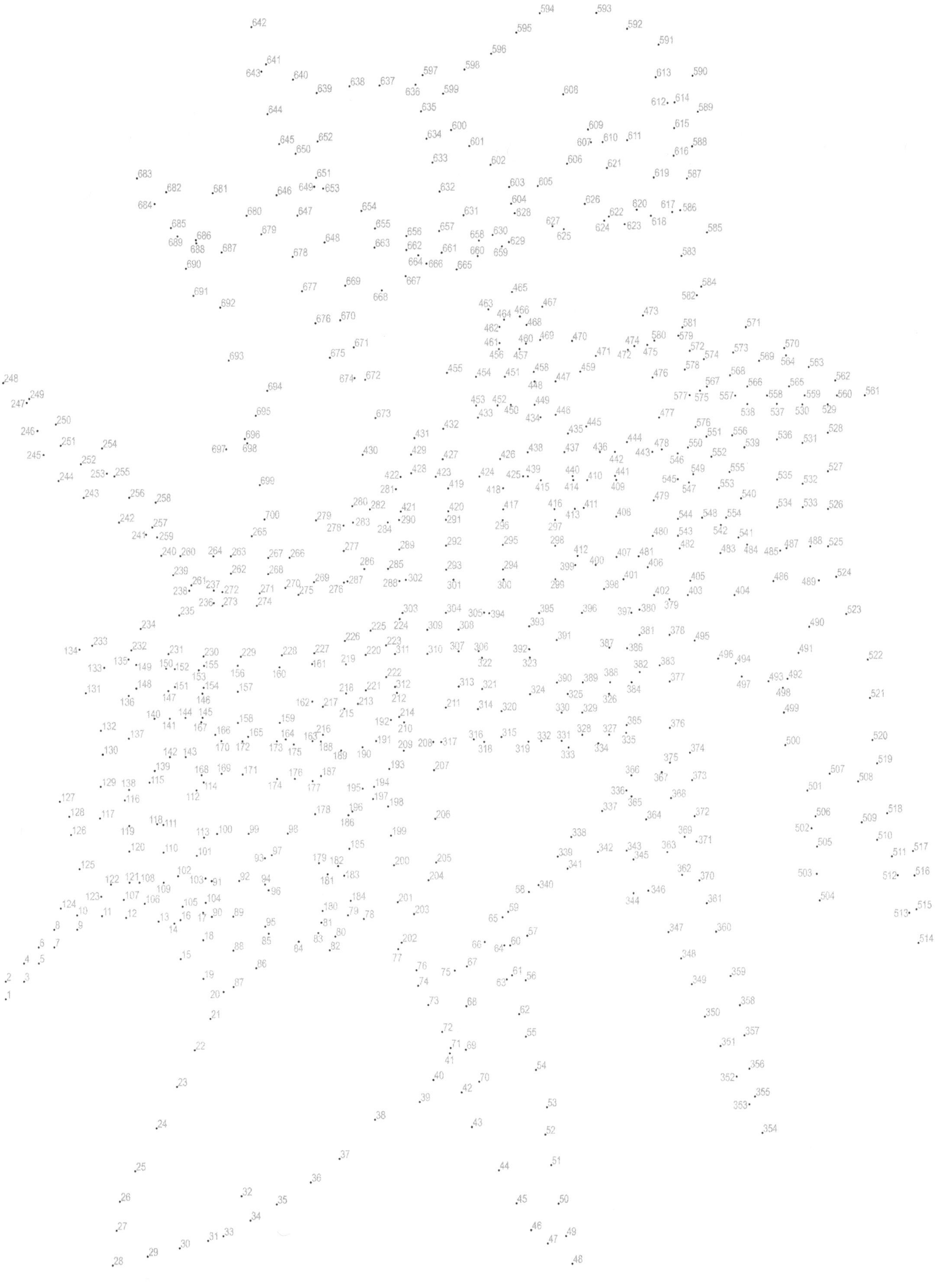

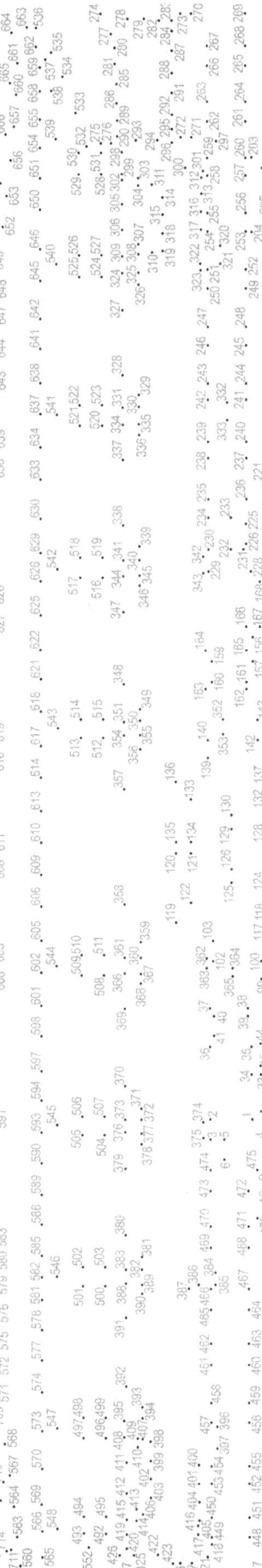

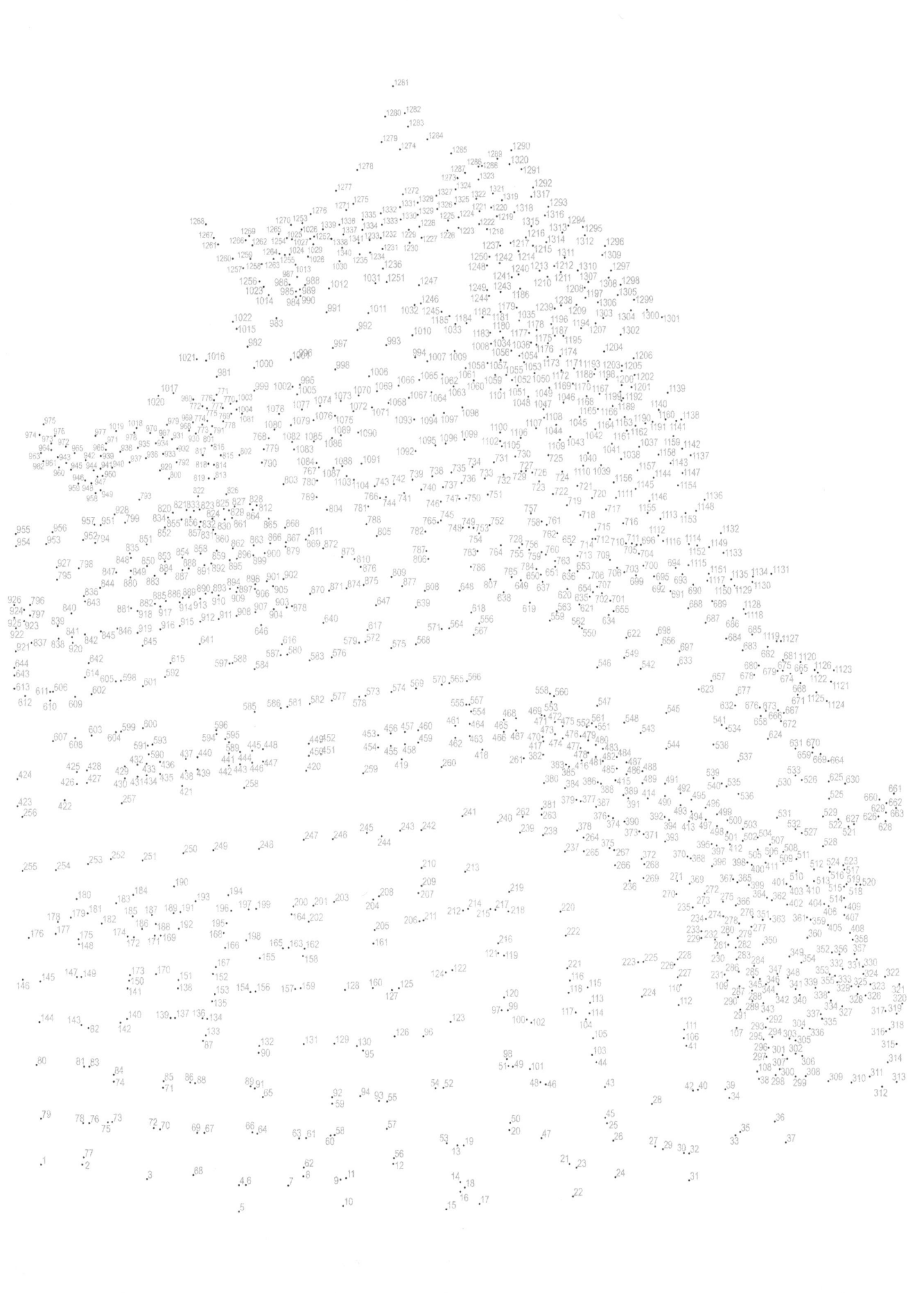

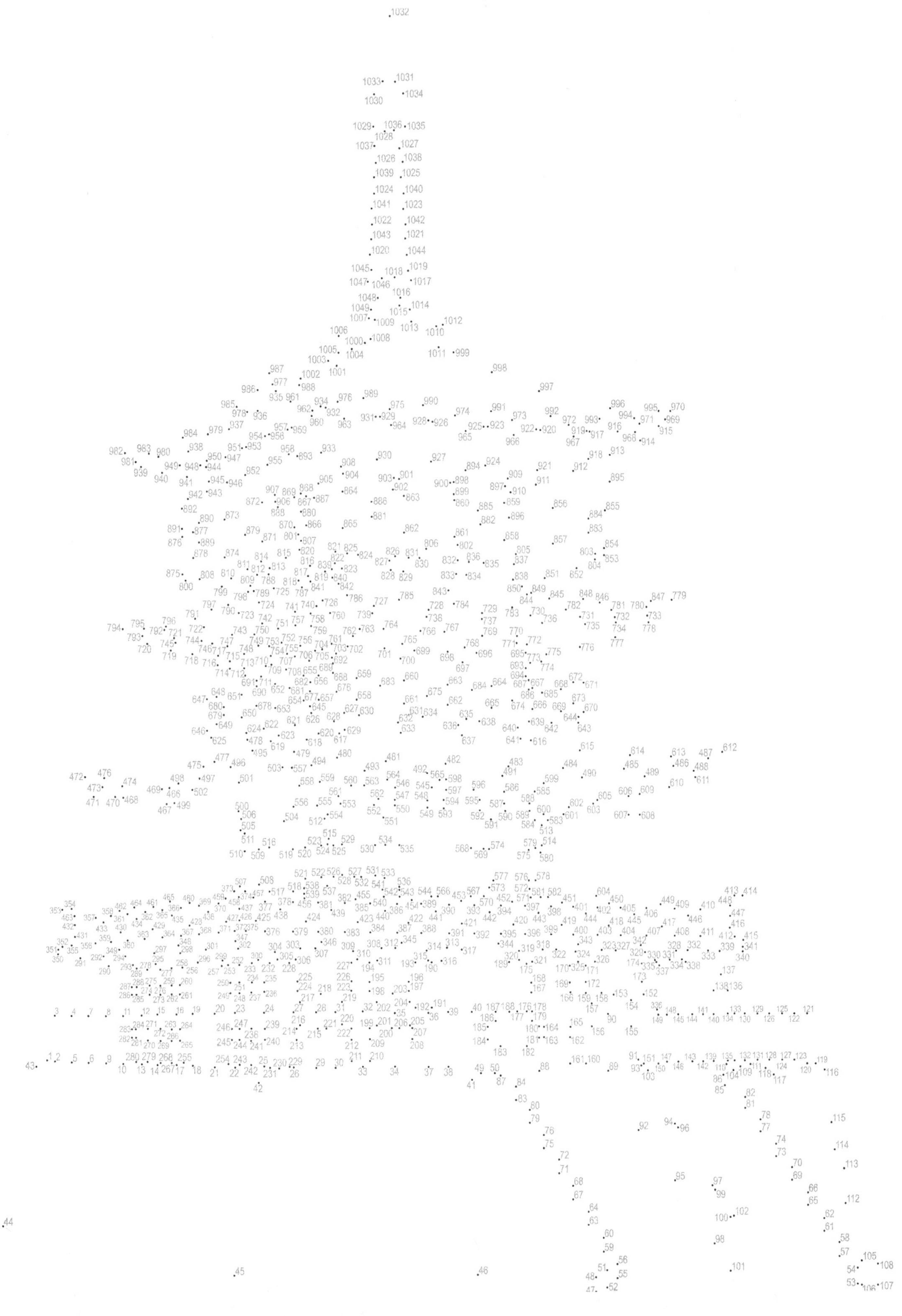

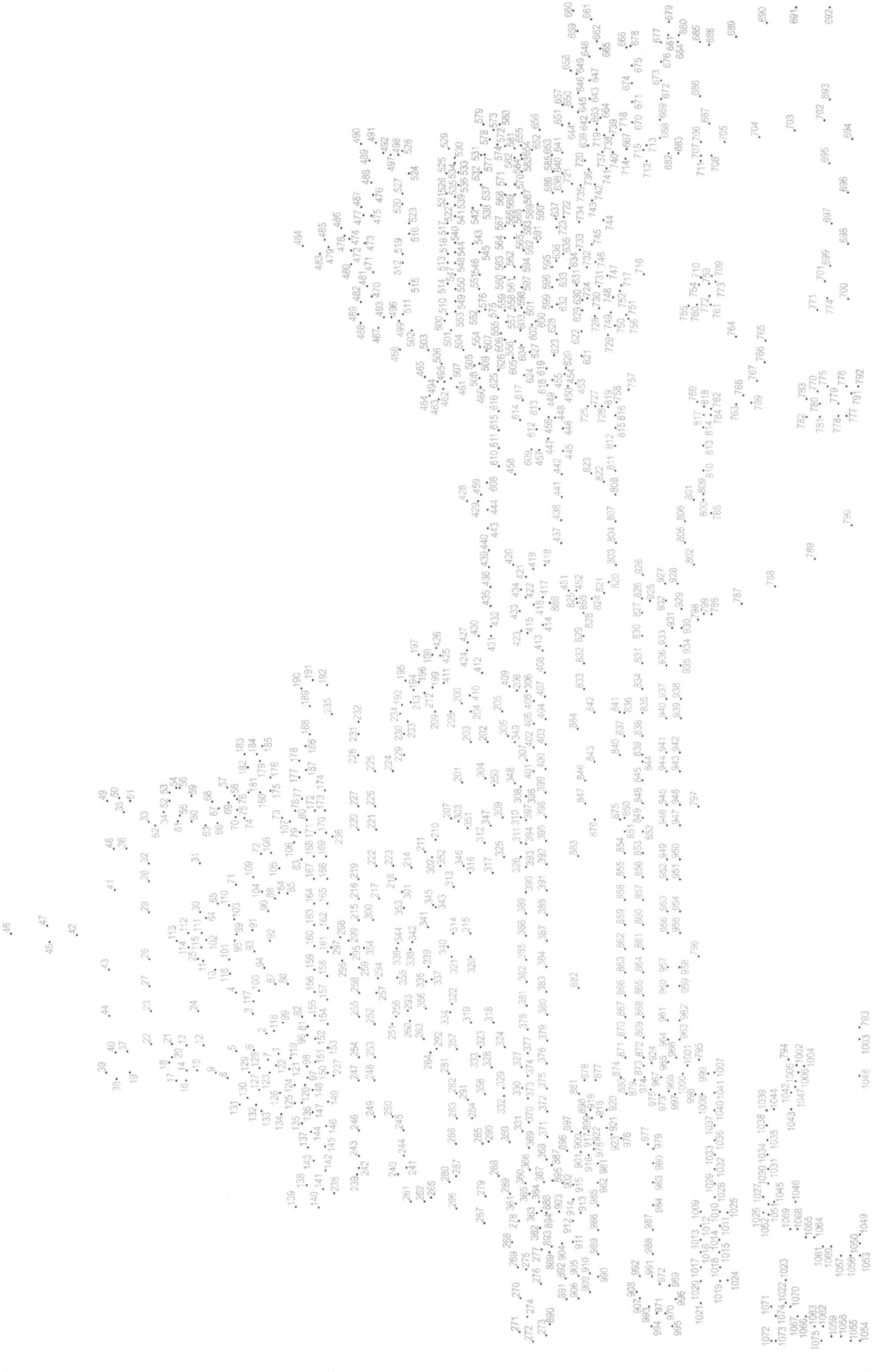

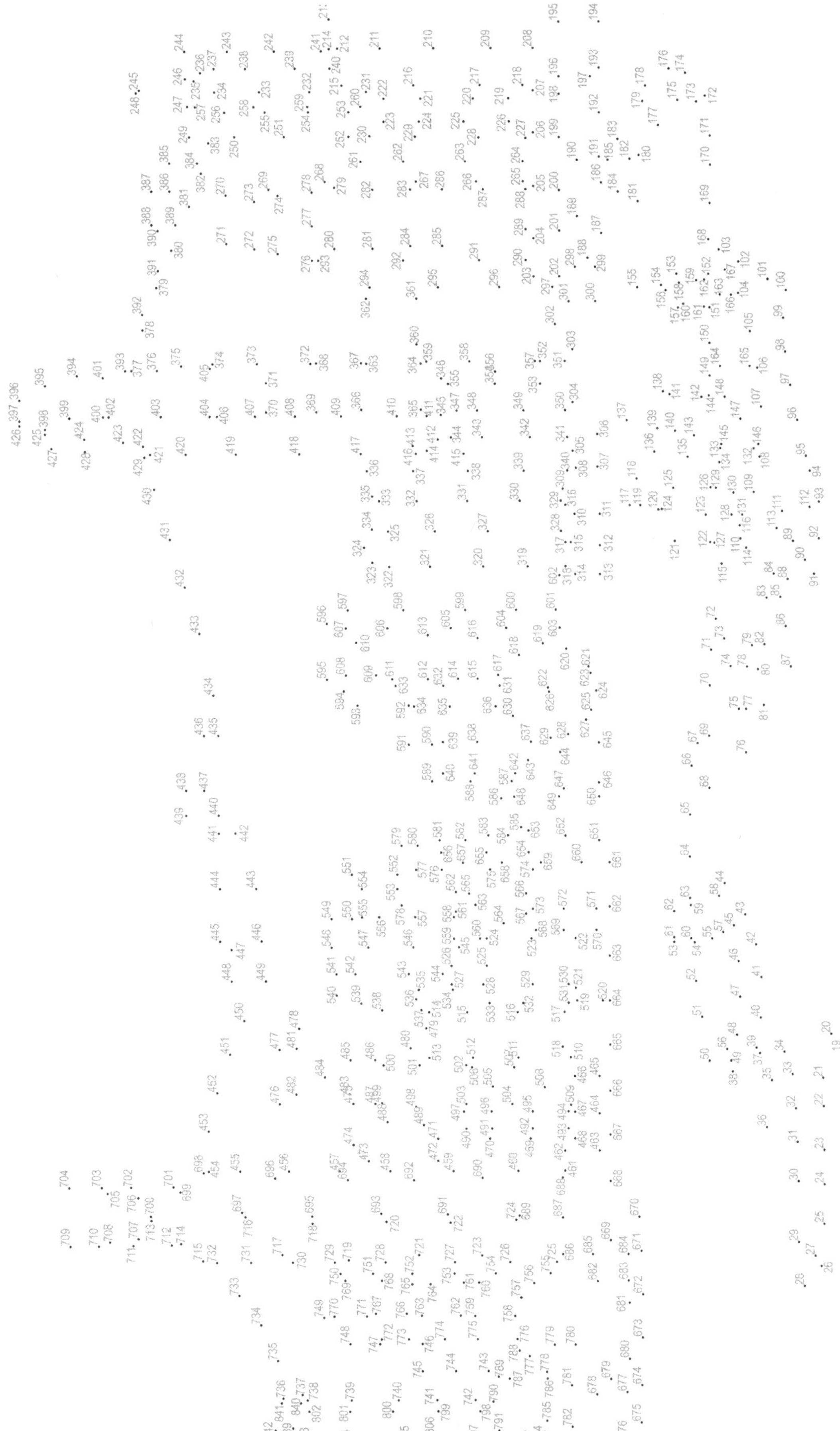

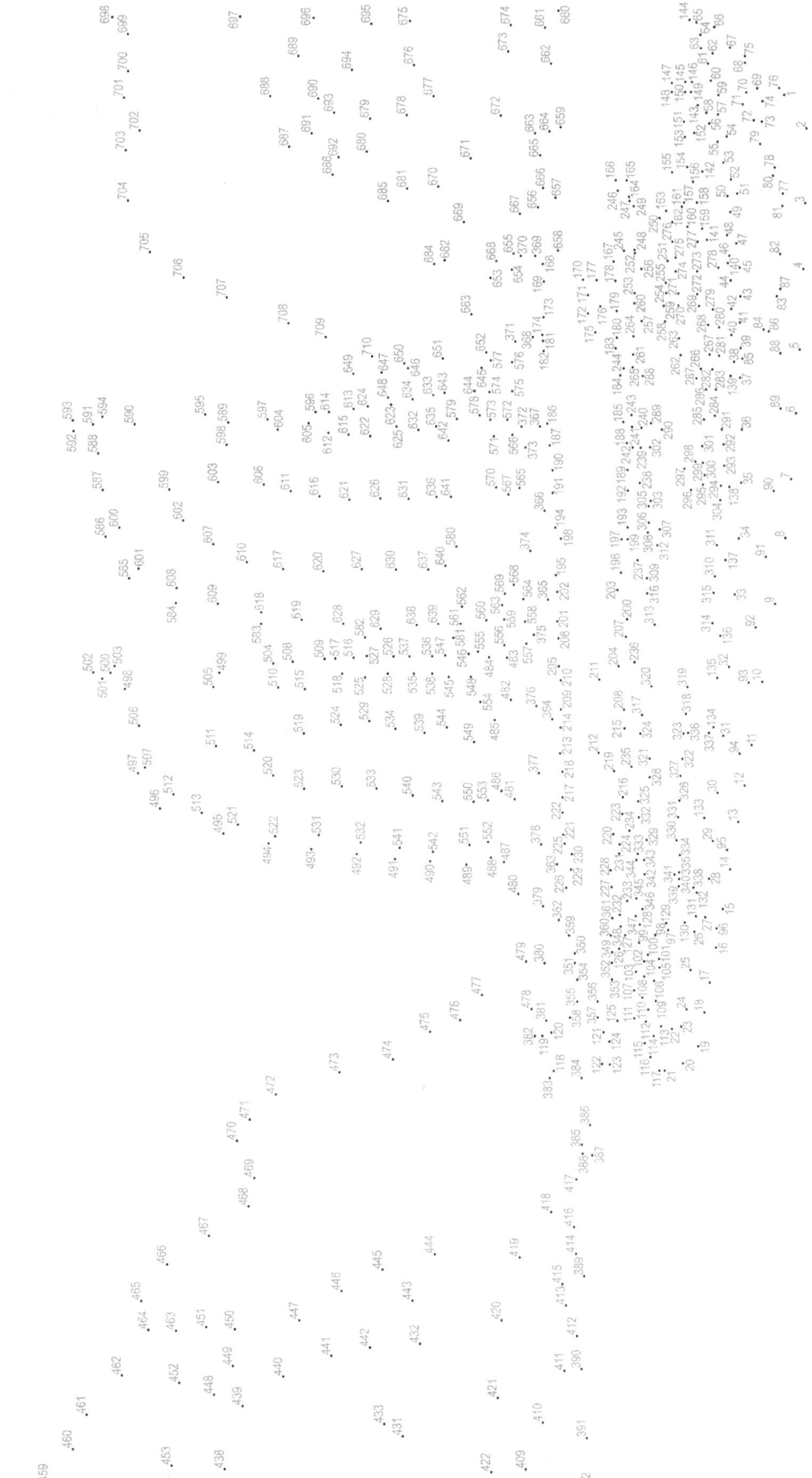

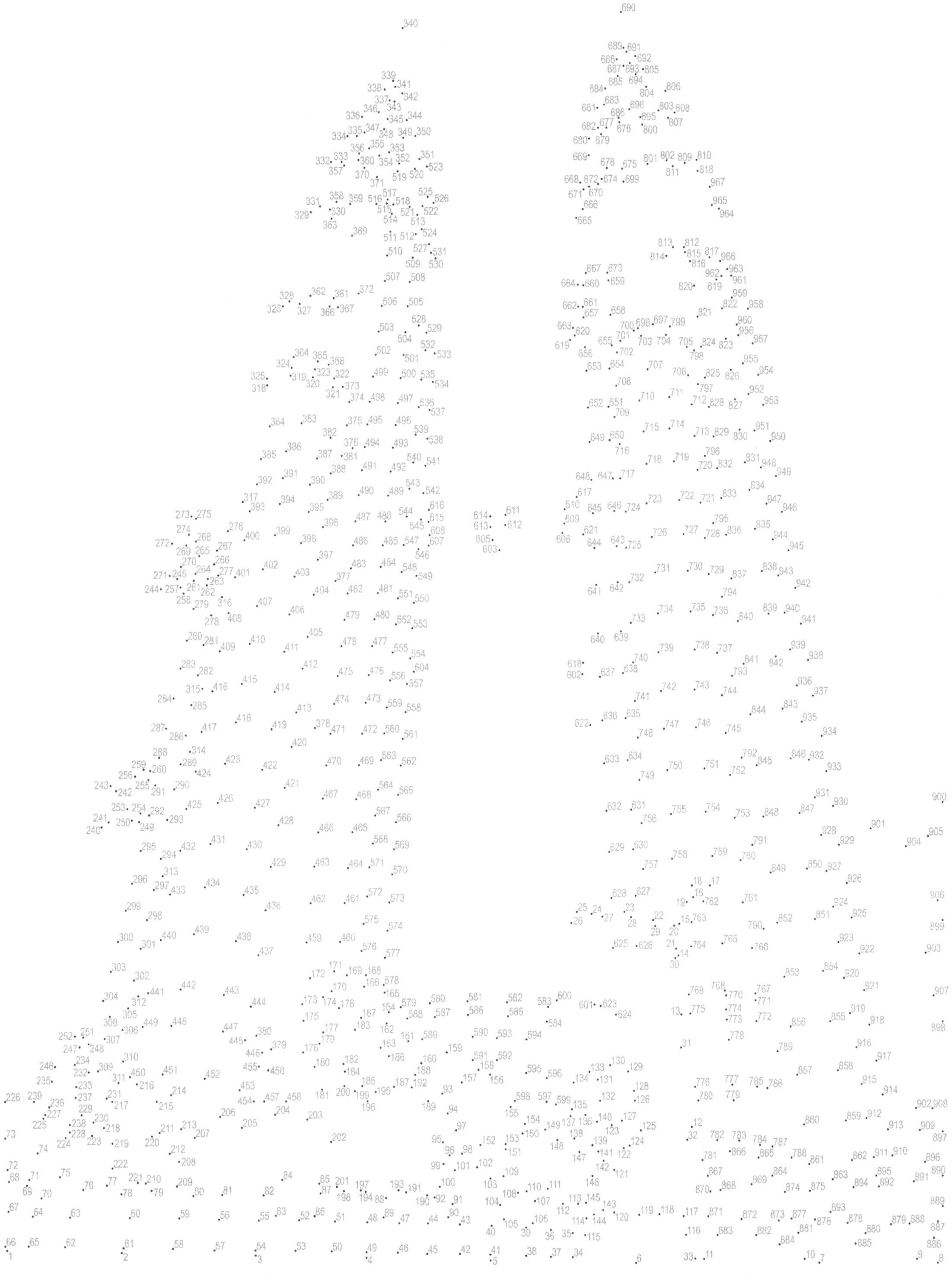

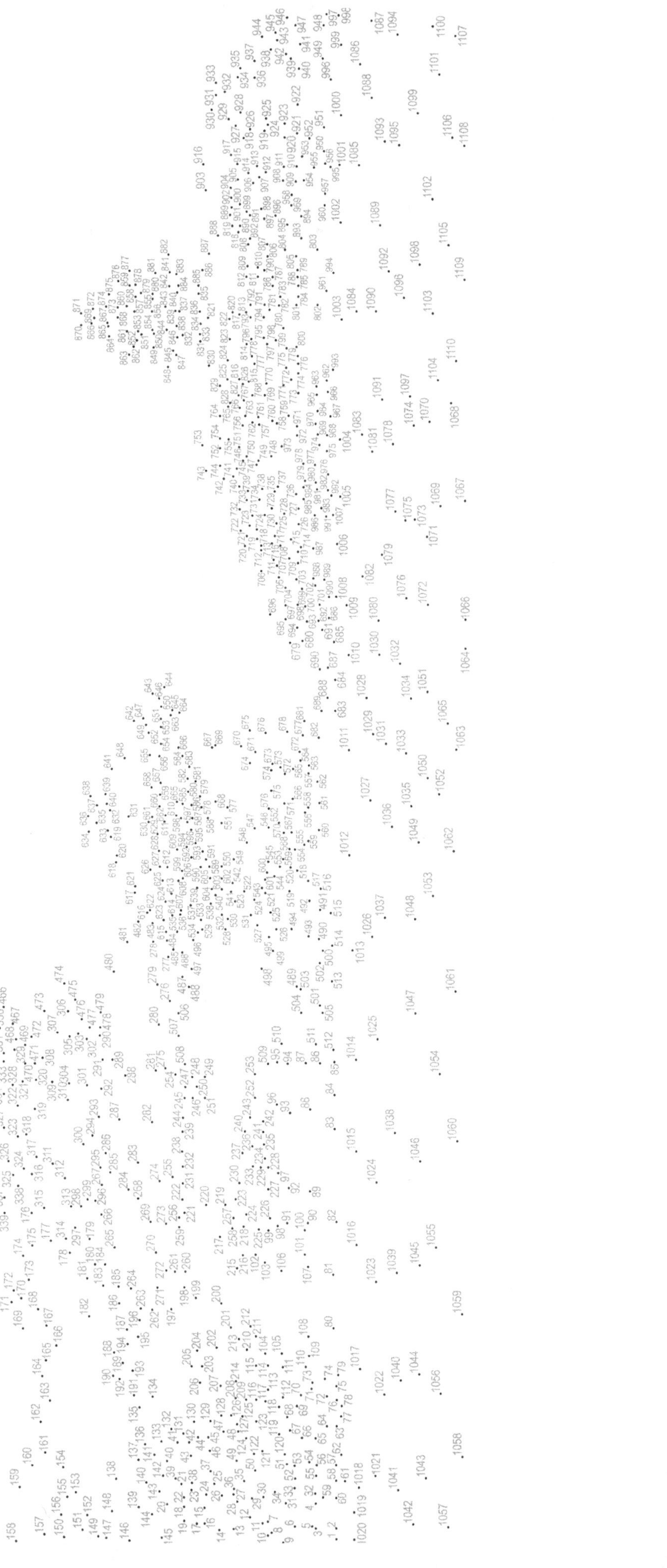

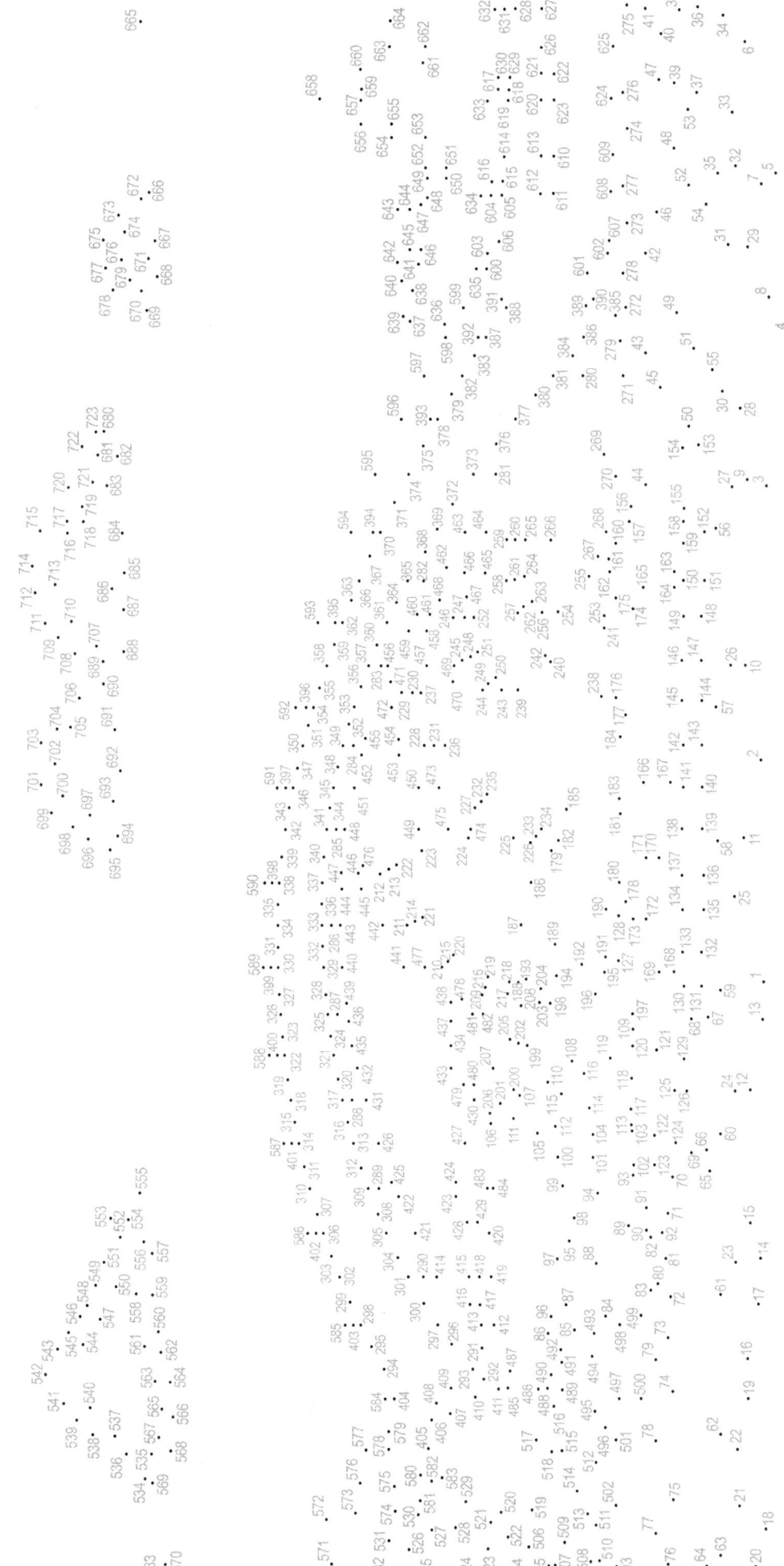

SOLUTIONS

Page 3: The Dome of the Rock, Jerusalem, Israel

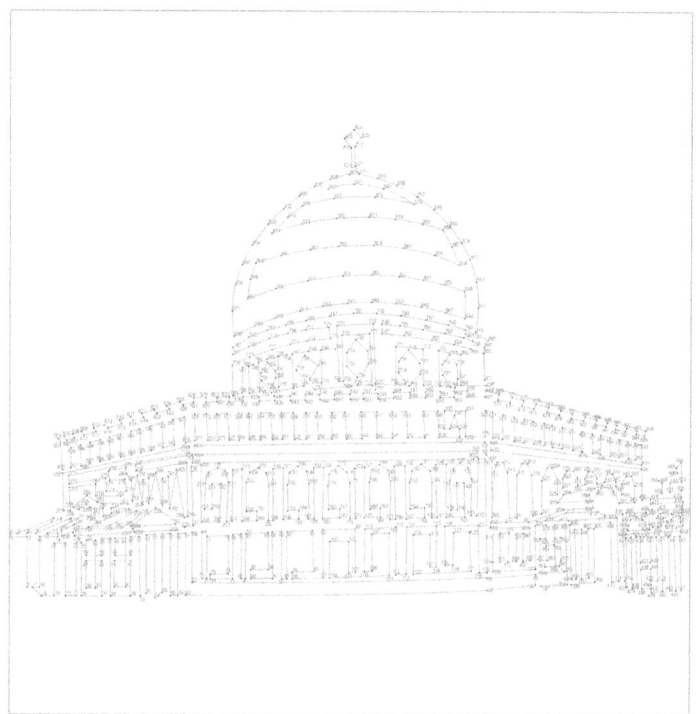

Page 5: Sultan Qaboos Grand Mosque, Muscat, Oman

Page 7: Burj Al Arab, Dubai, United Arab Emirates

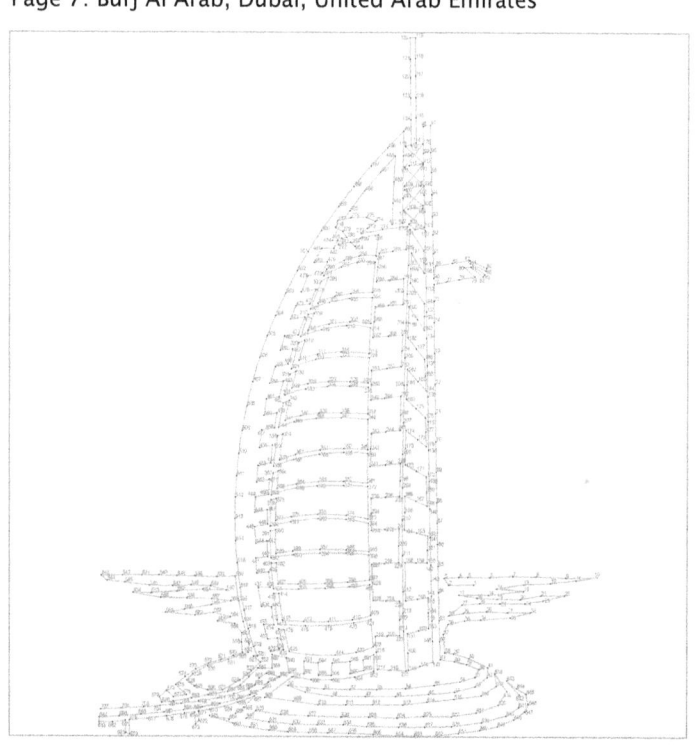

Page 9: Burj Khalifa, Dubai, United Arab Emirates

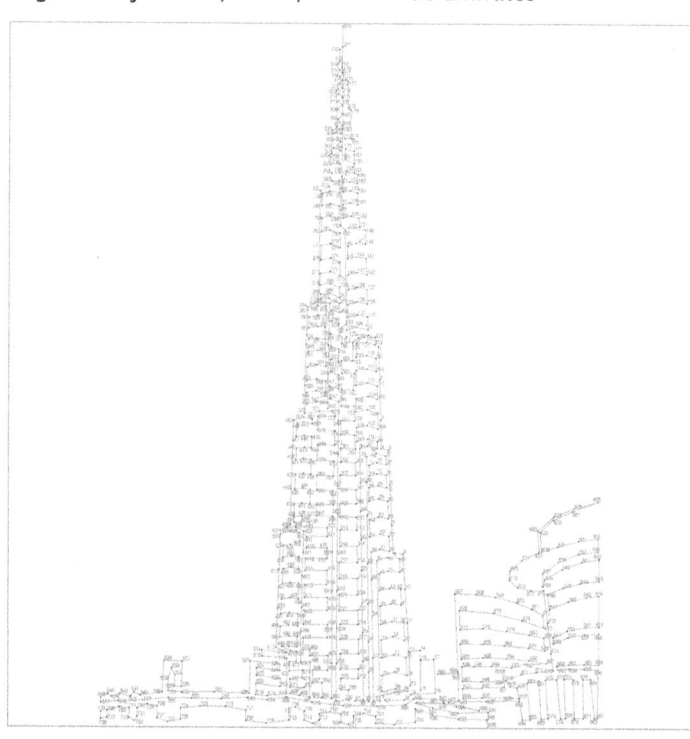

SOLUTIONS

Page 11: Chhatrapati Shivaji Terminus, Mumbai, India

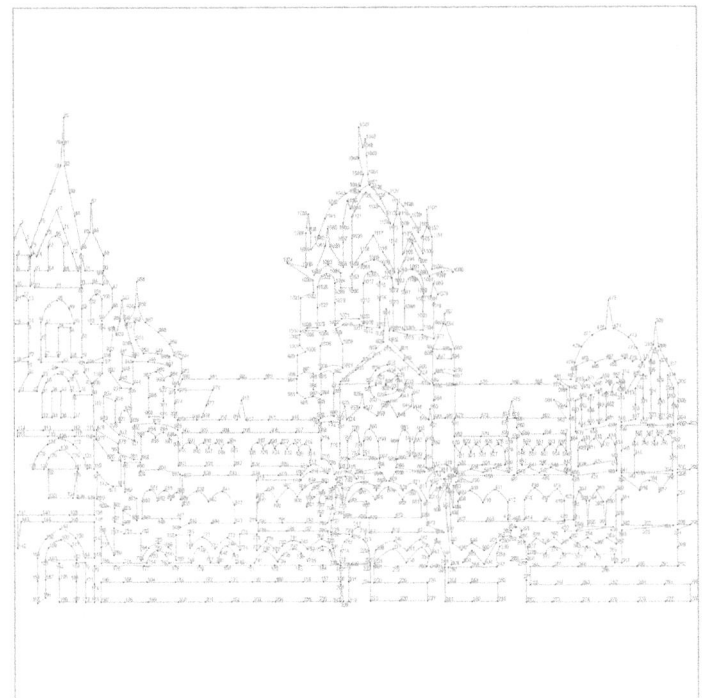

Page 13: Amer Fort, Rajasthan, India

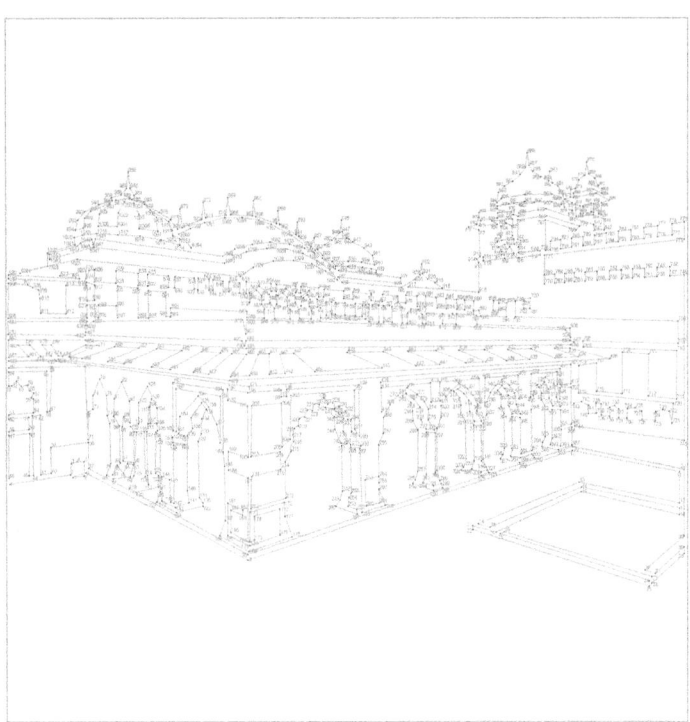

Page 15: Harmandir Sahib, Amritsar, India

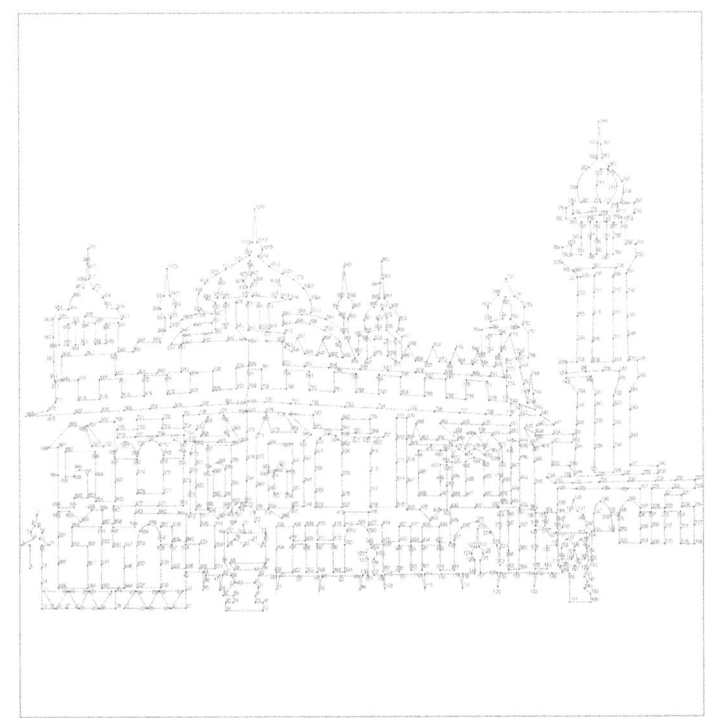

Page 17: Tiger's Nest, Paro Valley, Bhutan

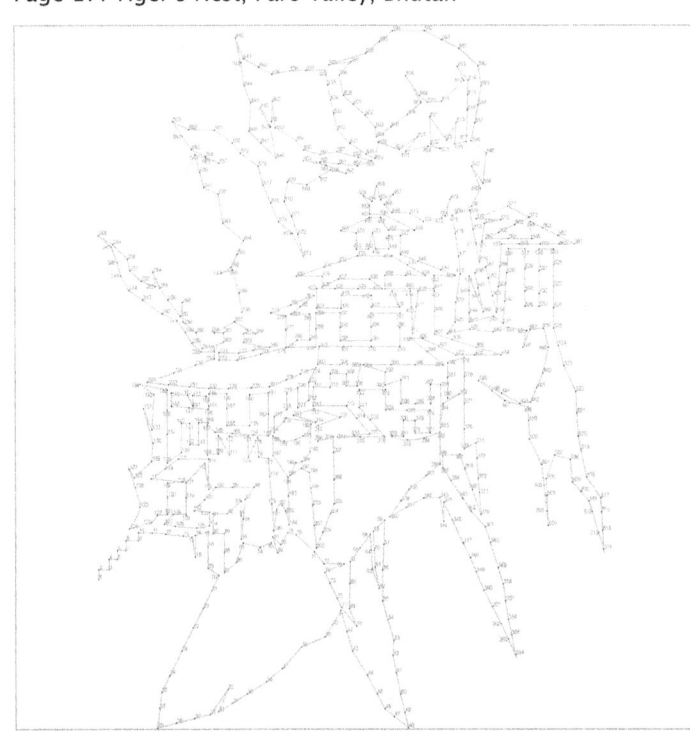

SOLUTIONS

Page 19: The Potala Palace, Lhasa, Tibet

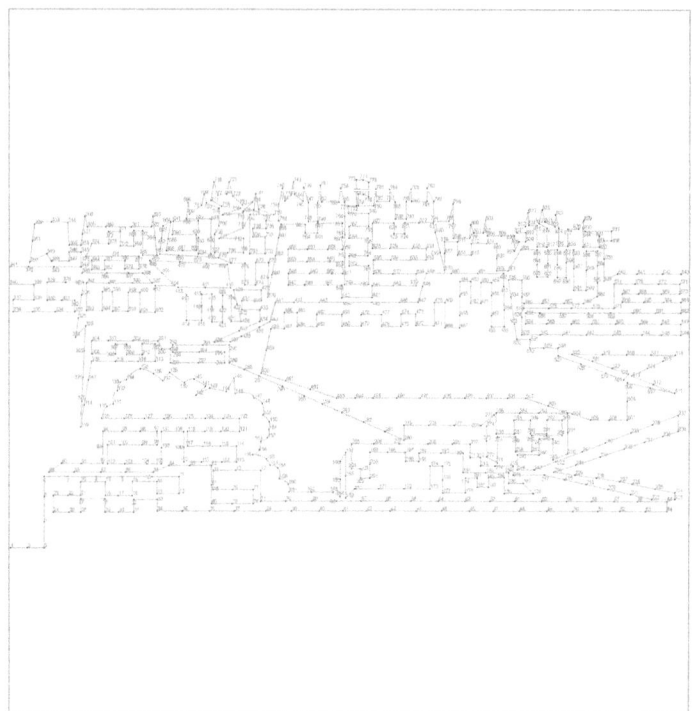

Page 21: The Summer Palace, Beijing, China

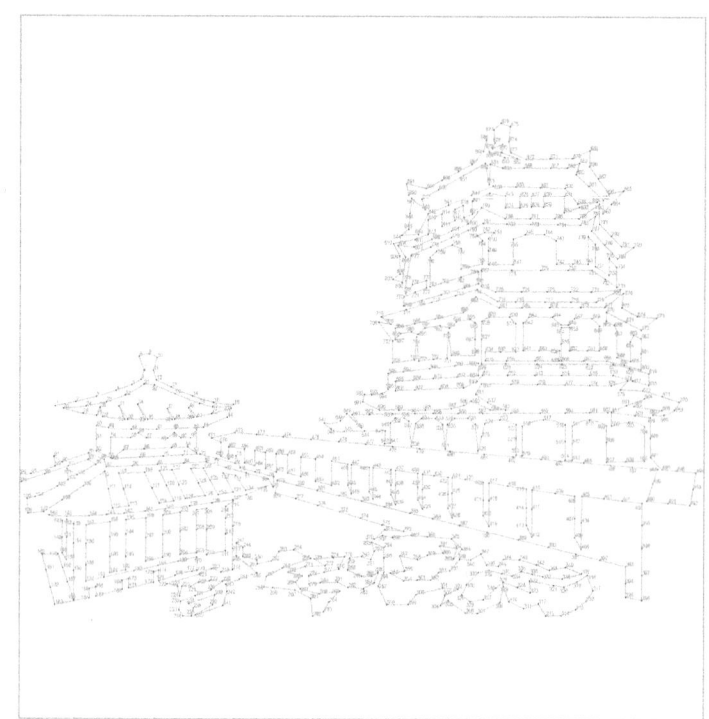

Page 23: The Mausoleum of Light, Shenyang, China

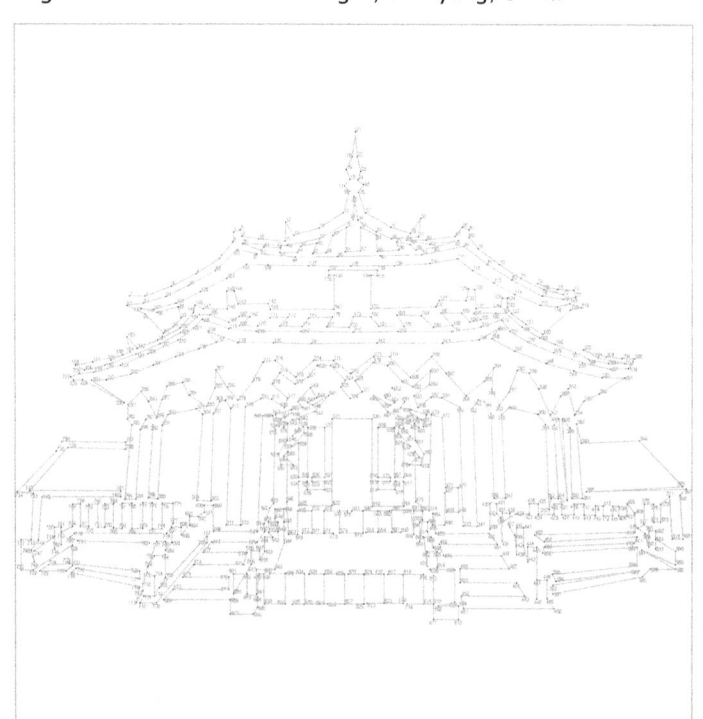

Page 25: Gyeongbokgung Palace, Seoul, South Korea

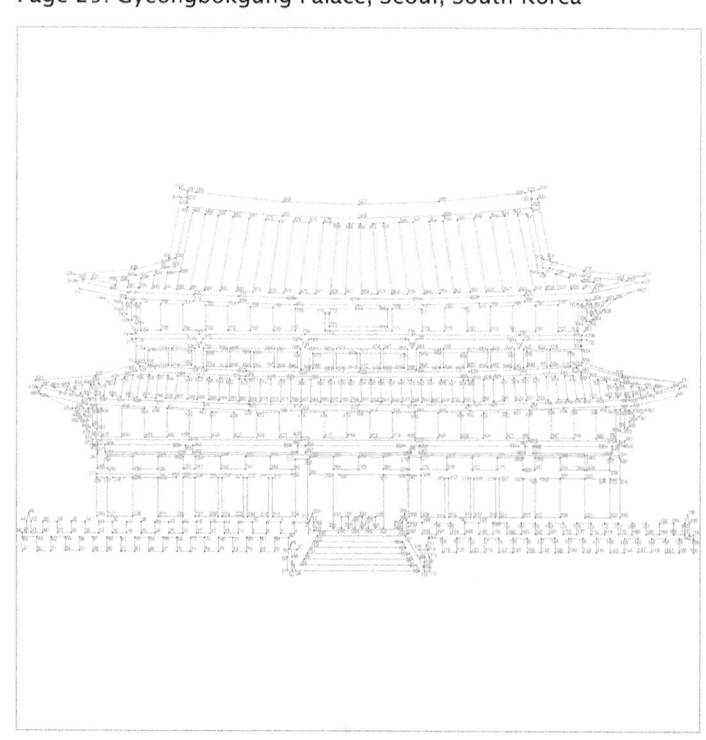

SOLUTIONS

Page 27: Imperial Palace, Tokyo, Japan

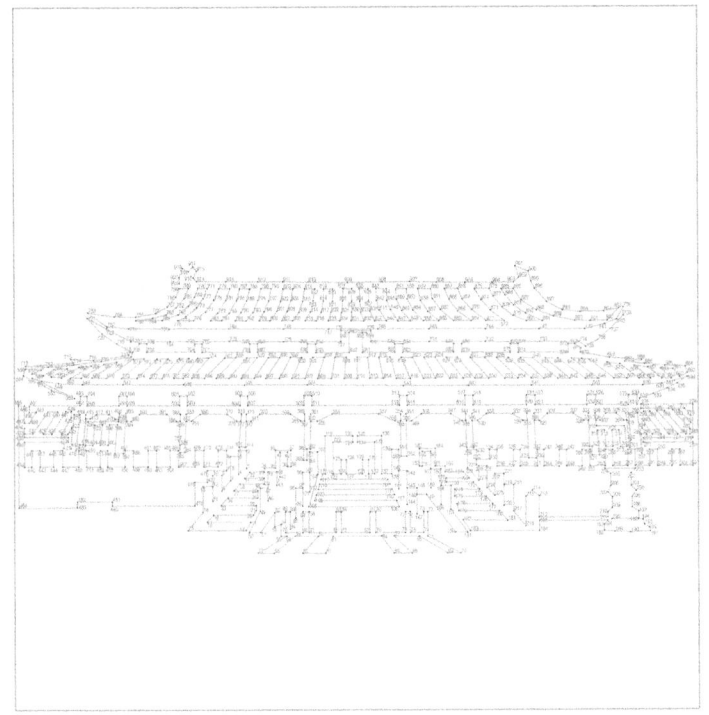

Page 29: Osaka Castle, Osaka, Japan

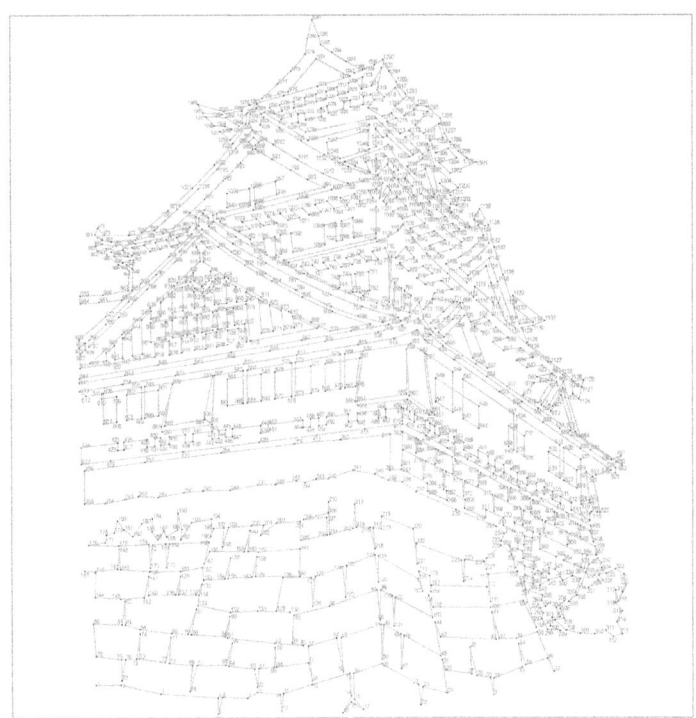

Page 31: Kinkakuji, Kyoto, Japan

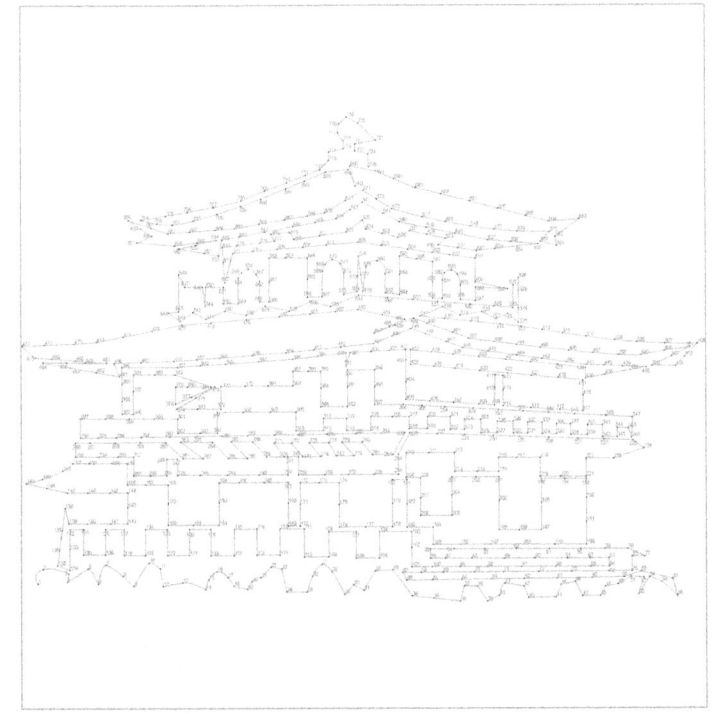

Page 33: Seiganto-ji Pagoda, Wakayama Prefecture, Japan

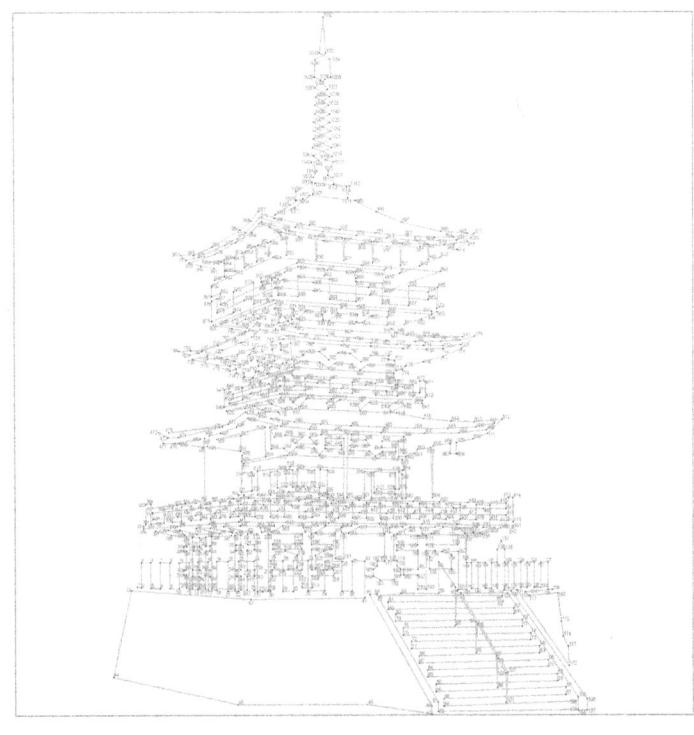

SOLUTIONS

Page 35: Fukuoka Castle, Fukuoka, Japan

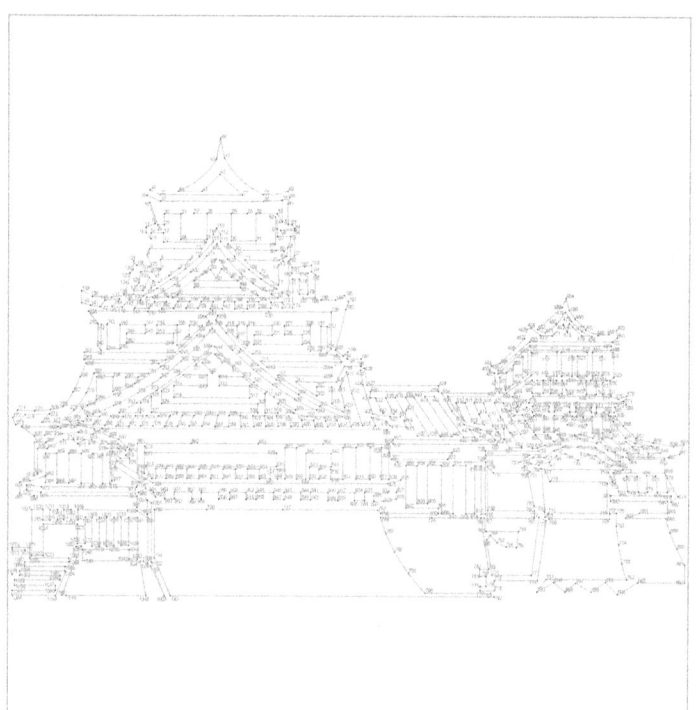

Page 37: The Hong Kong Skyline

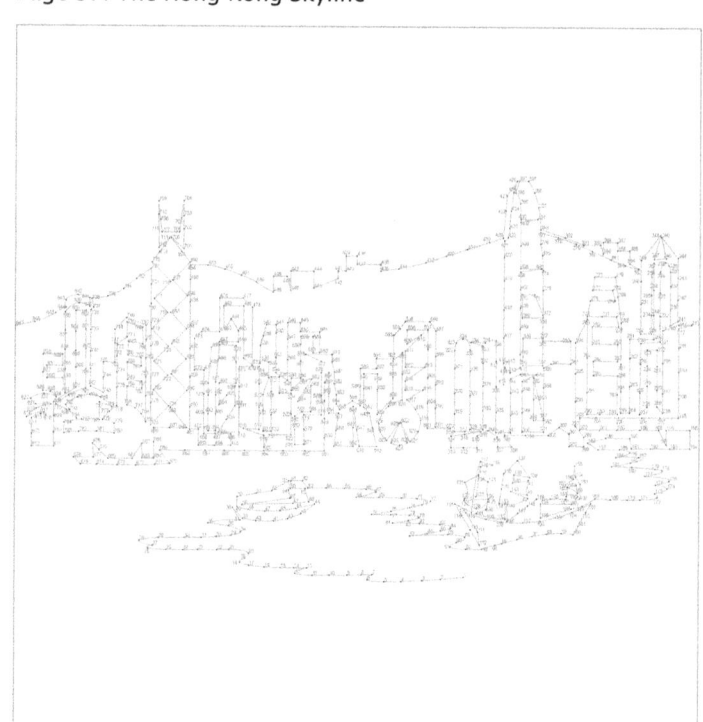

Page 39: Hạ Long Bay, Quảng Ninh Province, Vietnam

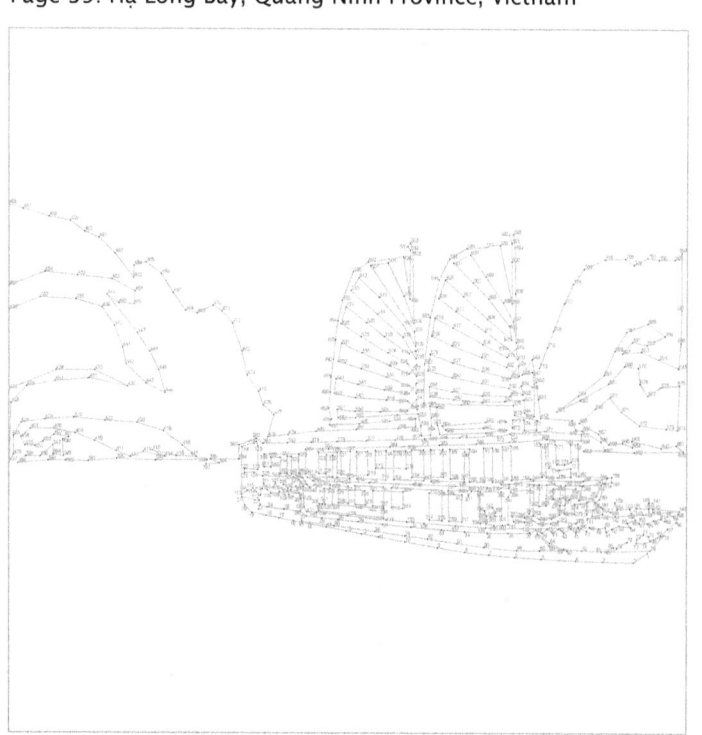

Page 41: Wat Phra Singh in Chiangmai, Thailand

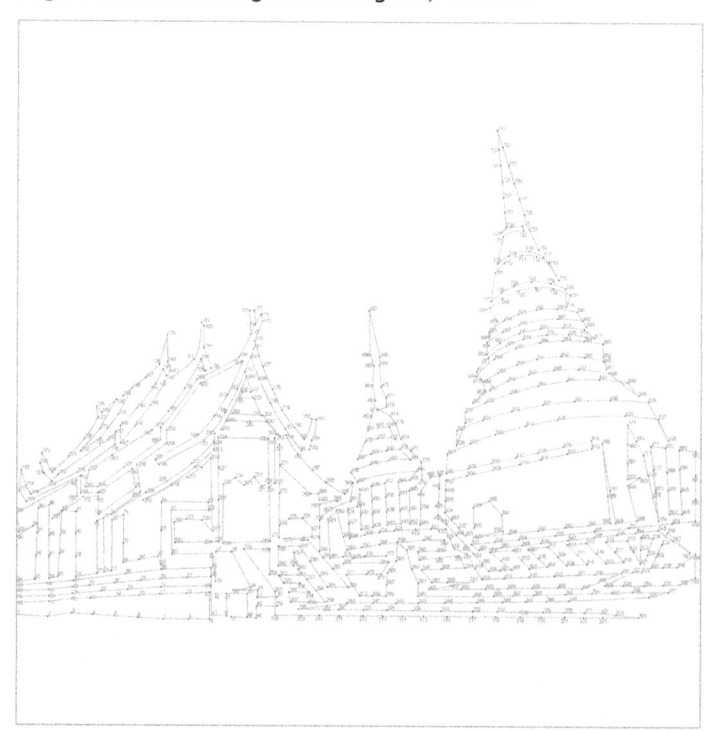

SOLUTIONS

Page 43: Shwedagon Pagoda, Yangon, Myanmar

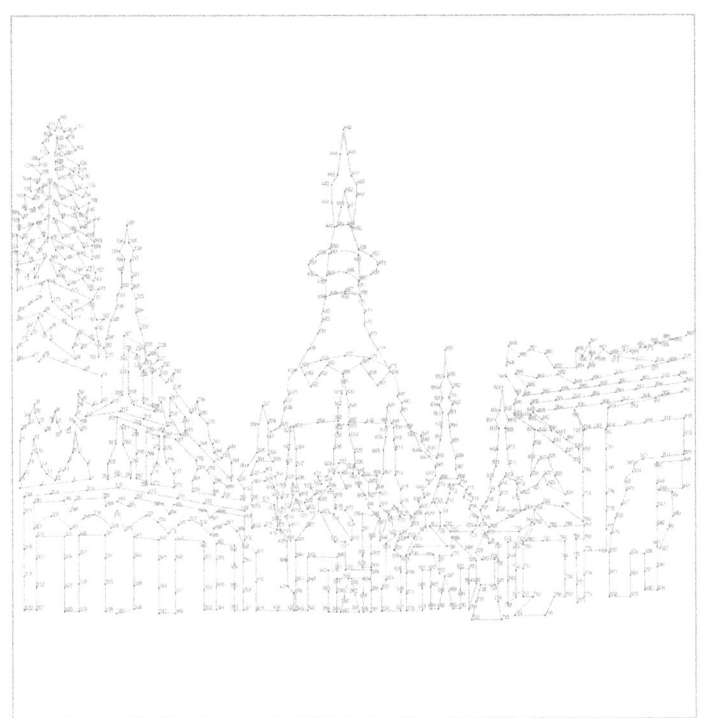

Page 45: Petronas Twin Towers, Kuala Lumpur, Malaysia

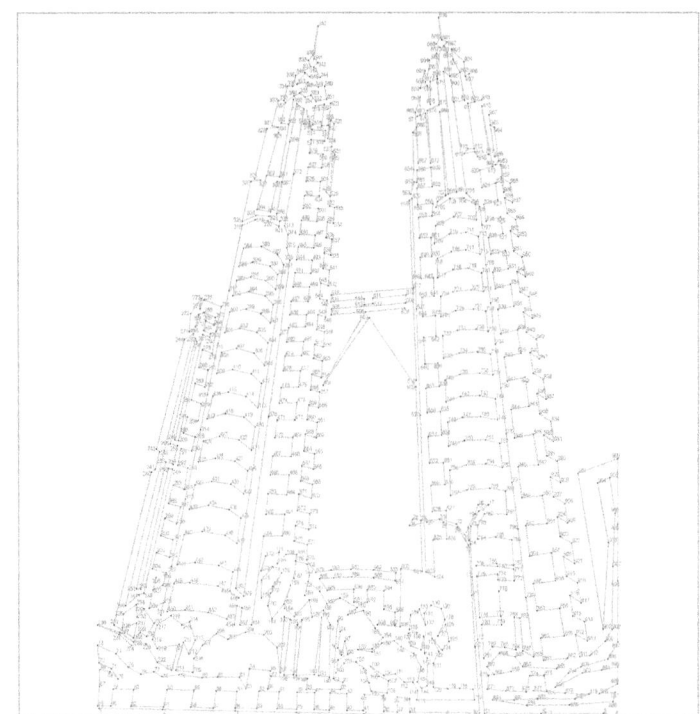

Page 47: Tanah Lot, Bali, Indonesia

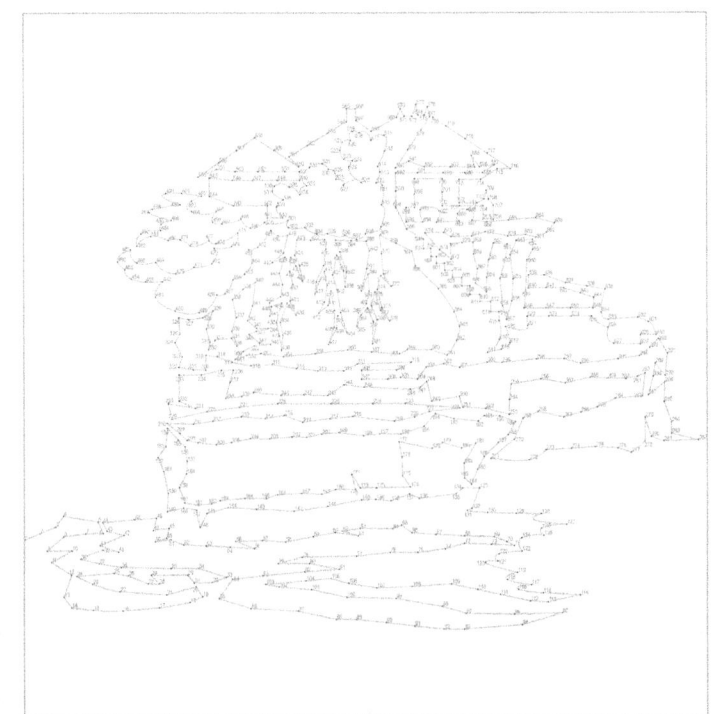

Page 49: Pura Ulun Danu Bratan, Bali, Indonesia

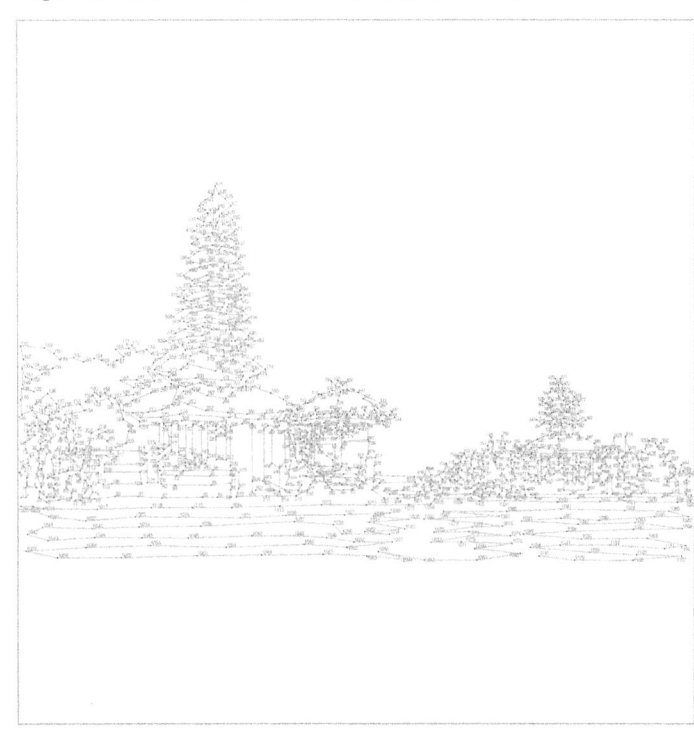

SOLUTIONS

Page 51: Sydney, Australia: Opera House & Harbour Bridge

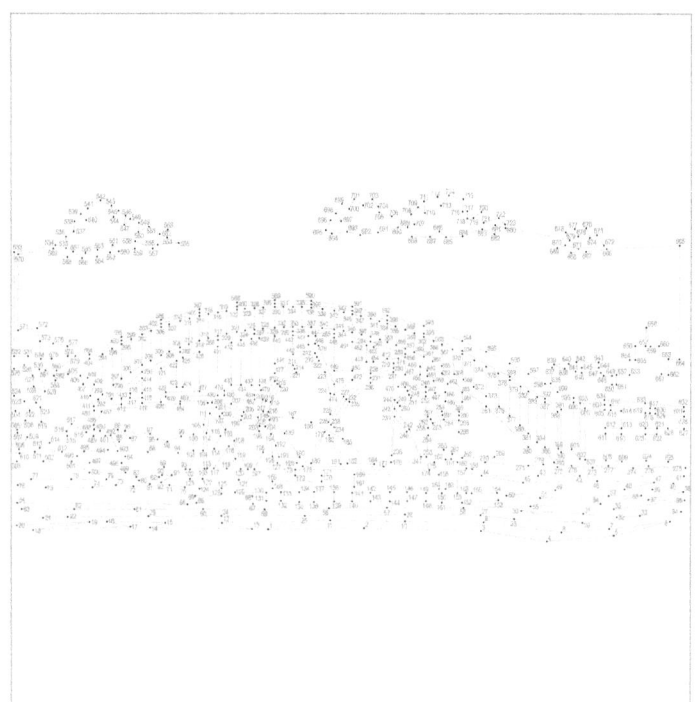

Page 53: Auckland, New Zealand: Skyline

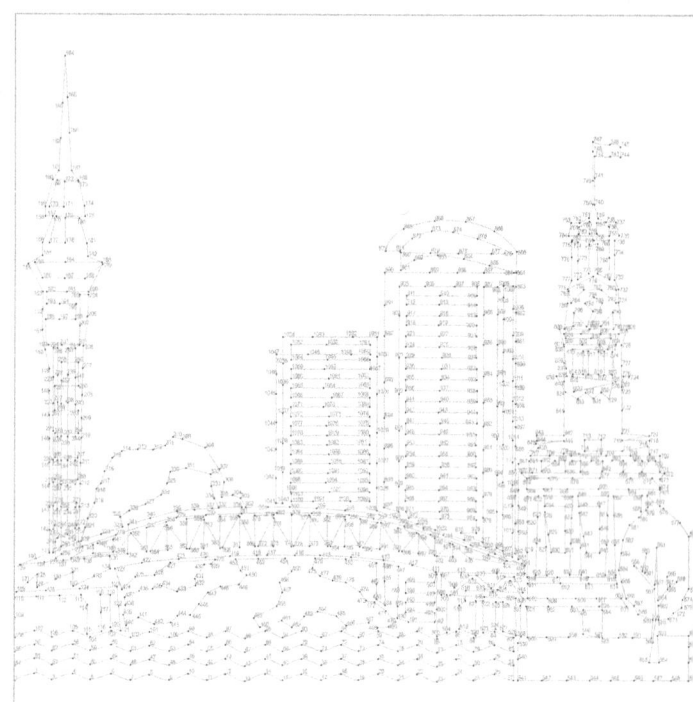

www.ingramcontent.com/pod-product-compliance
Lightning Source LLC
Chambersburg PA
CBHW082153230526
45467CB00044B/3254